A COLOURFUL AGE
Peter Sutton

To John

with warmest wishes

Peter Sutton

April 2023

A Colourful Age

Peter Sutton
Edited by Black Pear Press

First published in 2023 by Black Pear Press
www.blackpear.net
Copyright © Peter Sutton

ISBN 978-1-913418-76-2

Cover image by Tony Judge & DALL·E 2
Cover design by Black Pear Press

Black Pear Press

Preface

Having published my short collection *Elgar Country* in 2022, the Black Pear Press has kindly agreed to publish this longer set of poems in 2023. They have been written over the preceding seven years and are arranged in four sections: 'Colour Vision', which splits the world into the colours of the rainbow, 'Belief', which reflects on how we try in our small ways to make sense of existence, 'Family', which is topped and tailed by poems written for my two granddaughters but is otherwise not chiefly autobiographical, and 'Old Age', which does draw heavily on my own experience. An awareness of colours persists throughout.

The majority of the poems are written in formal verse, that is to say that they follow a strict pattern of rhythm and rhyme, and they are designed to be read aloud. Where there is no rhyme at the end of a line, there will usually be a rhyme within the line, or at least a regular number of syllables and stresses. I also use alliteration, in which several stressed words in a line begin with the same sound. It is a practice inherited from Old and Middle English which has been in my head ever since I translated the great medieval work *Piers Plowman* into modern alliterative verse a decade ago.

The use of formal verse is purely my preference, and I say nothing against free, unrhymed verse, which can also contain powerful imagery and rhythms, assonance and alliteration, and can express the writer's intention with pin-point accuracy. However, I generally find the challenge of form more satisfying. It obliges me to hunt for words and phrases that match both the form I have chosen and my meaning, both of which may be changed and enriched by the very process of hunting.

I hope that readers will enjoy the results of my quest and will find something in my vision of our colourful age that resonates with them.

Contents

Colour Vision

The Red Lion

A certain public house which I frequent,
a fusty place that rests in peace beside a church,
is bent with age and creaks and groans as spreading roots
and water courses swell and shift and die.

The hostess, clad in madder cardy, ambles in
when custom calls, dispensing headless pints of ale,
responding to enquiries with a stunted nod,
invariably short of cash and breath.

If asked she can turn out a wilted cheese or ham
on brown that's made from flour sacks or white that melts
to nothing but a twist of old man's beard, as did
her mother's mother's mother's mother's dam.

For generations they upheld the endless round
as tapsters to the village till some fancy folk
requested foreign lagers, rosé wines and meals,
and asked for decaf coffee and mint tea.

The landlord told them where to go, and one by one,
all but a few, they vanished and he cursed the trade
inherited from forebears, drank the profits dry,
and ran off with the woman from next door.

But that was years ago, since when his wife has clung
to hope and long tradition in the public bar,
abandoning the snug to stacks of broken chairs
and cobwebbed crates of ales no longer made.

Already loving tendrils have crept in and curled
their arms around the photos of the cricket team
and comrades in their khaki kit, moustachioed,
and run-down, rusted, clockwork children's toys.

There are a son and daughter somewhere in the world, but do they want to strip the building, clear the weeds, set out umbrellas, change the kitchen, fit new pumps and serve red curries, tacos, noodles? No.

Self-portrait

I draw a red vee like a dart as grotesque as my chin,
above it another, a beak that is sharp like a rook,
a twin of the first which ensures I'm as ugly as sin.
I look like a crook.

I add in an upside-down vee to enhance the bent look,
between the two others, a door-stepping, barbaric grin,
a blackguard, a villain, a thief in a comic-strip book.

Two more vees above them, two eyebrows uplifted and thin,
like upside-down legs, just a tick, just a tiny wee hook,
and red eyes beneath them, as mean and as sharp as a pin.
I look like a crook.

Tomato Licence

Do not ignore this red alert.

Your growing licence has expired
and you are now at urgent risk
of prosecution, prison, fines
and civil action in the courts
if any noxious wayward plants
for which you are responsible,
or fruit thereof, should such arise—
tomato is a fruit in law—
cause intestinal damage, hurt,
material, pecuniary,
or physical or mental harm,
distress, discomfort and/or loss
to innocent third parties.

It is therefore essential that
you register online and state
how many and what kind of plants
you entertain, maintain and keep
and other details that we may
require, request, demand and store
regarding health and diet, age,
your chosen gender, children, pets,
your education, income, debts,
your place of birth and parentage,
employment history, politics,
religious faith, relationships,
your alcohol consumption, drugs,
your social media likes, your apps,
TV shows, music, websites, films,
your hobbies, hopes and groundless fears.

Your data will be safe with us.

Red

Red is propitious.

Red is malicious.

Flags are red, Watneys Red, Up the reds!

Rusty red, fusty red, poxy red.

Seeing red, sun is red, sea of red.

Cheque is red, roses red, stop it's red.

Penny red, ruby red, knickers red.

Red is for weddings.

Red's for beheadings.

A Colourful Childhood

When I grew up I thought Bromley was blue,
though the Quaggy was pisspot brown,
and Orpington was buff,
which made good sense
especially if you kept hens.

Sevenoaks was green,
which I swear it was,
Eltham was puce,
the shade of a shopfront, name long lost,
and Sidcup was sunrise yellow,
the end of the bus line,
except when one
went under the bridge
and lost its top
because the driver forgot.

And London itself, old London Town,
round the Tower, Tower Green,
was redbreast, redcoat, Chelsea red,
and the Crays were grey,
and somewhere was orange,
and where I hated school every day
was off the end of the rainbow.

Art Class

A woman is painting a tangle of snakes inside a cube,
a lattice of tongues,
not painting the snakes but a picture of snakes,
of zigzagging, second-hand strakes.

And a man is cutting a shape from a sheet the size of a shroud,
the shape of a girl.
He pegs the shape to a frame like a skin,
a drum to be played with a brush.

He is staring bleakly at plastic heads in line astern
like buses in town.
The cauliflower brains inside show through,
the venomous thoughts in the heads.

He is flicking his painterly thoughts at the sheet, citrine thoughts
of lemon and lime,
marmalade, gooseberry, apricot,
the colours of firelight and jam.

I gaze at the woman who is painting the snakes and see herself,
her daughter and child,
the women packed tightly like Russian dolls,
inside, inside, inside.

Till I look at the tubes of pavement turds, the heads and the shroud,
and count their days,
the fungi, the ochre, the tan and the dun,
and bury my thoughts underground.

Sugar

From the strong there came forth sweetness,
from the factory by the river
tipping, mashing, crushing pectals
hard as nails

Heave, my hearties, cast off for'ard
haul away from waves and greetings,
last words, leavings, tying knots and
calling rails

To Norroway, to Norroway
Flying Dutchman, Kursk, Titanic,
Mary Rose, Free Enterprise and
raging gales

Leo prowls the star-crossed heavens
Lea hunts the brassy harbour
ware the ship of fools and sweeties
twitching tails

Orange

Jaffa orange, juicy orange, Seville orange, navel orange.

Still orange, sparkling orange, breakfast orange, gin and orange.

Pithy orange, pippy orange, peel an orange, pee is orange.

Bright orange, blood orange, prison orange, Agent Orange.

Orange is bitter and orange is sweet.

Colour Wheel

Red chilli-pepper opposite green,
greenhorn green, Fenian green,
blue-vein challenging stinking bishop,
Old Orange flutes v. blaue Blume,
blooming gloomy highbrow humour,
and eggplant laughing at egghead yoke,
indigo upping its pin-pricked arms
and jousting with jolly old jaundice.

And the in-betweens sneak in between,
reddish yellow Cuban chunks,
yellowy bluey arty chokes,
and bluish reddish sprouting spears.
Stand away, green!
Hands off now, red!

Silver Gilt

The bright polished sheen
of the xanthic moon
has been rubbed raw
by thick rubber boots.

The gold that glisters,
glory of the gods,
bubbles in the furnace of
the lab-coated mind.

While long human limbs
reach for the stars,
for the breathless planets,
and the answer why.

But Martians are here,
gilded, crested, bronzed and martial
marshals marching, swearing that
they are in command.

Skirting the Edge

I am walking around the rim
gingerly, minding where I put
my feet,

avoiding sulphurous, broken ground
where badly healed old wounds and scars
stand proud,

and watching for renewed outbursts,
unstable fractures, sudden slides
and shards.

I have covered my nose and mouth
with a mask that I hope will hide
my fear,

but my yellowy eyes reveal
the noxious nature of the airs
that rise

through fissures in the lava flow
from overheated gases deep
inside,

which thrust up to the surface of
the febrile earth, the coping of
the mind.

A fault, they say, a clash of worlds,
a chemical imbalance in
the brain.

Yellow

Brimstone yellow, belly yellow, skin yellow, plum yellow.

Sunny yellow, sickly yellow, streak of yellow, Case Yellow.

Autumn yellow, turning yellow, mellow yellow, saffron yellow.

Yellow is craven, yellow is shallow.

Yellow is sunshine, yellow is hallow.

Tidy World

I'm tidying, trimming the parchmented shrubs,
ejecting the snails from petunia tubs,
dead-heading the senescent, long-legged rose,
expelling the weeds from the haricots,
perfecting the future, pruning the past,
but leaving the glaucous leaf-mould till last,
allowing the buffos their moment of rest,
and sparing the hedge where the song-birds nest.

In my next avatar when I am the tsar,
I shall shake the paw of a gold labrador,
rub noses and fins with canny dolphins,
shake octopus graduands by the hands,
go hunting the snark with a learned shark,
swap smart bons mots with inquisitive crows,
sing ditties with whales as we thrash our tails,
and pluck jaundiced fleas from bemused chimpanzees.

But in this life I've a much bigger brain
than these omophagous friends can attain.
I also tidy the few last remains
of forests and meadows and wetlands and plains,
I govern the beasts of land, sea and air,
I pick and choose what to grow, what to wear,
I speak through music and pictures and rhyme,
and hunt for how to unravel space-time.

I am without doubt the top of the tree,
the acme of natural selection,
aggressive, divisive, ruthless and free—
don't I manage my world to perfection?

To the Lighthouse

Come, they screech, where clouded sea meets loaded sky,
wreckers ululating through a tattered cloud,
heaving, hauling, grappling, yawling, morbid, sly
chartreuse floozies, banshees, kelpies, Neptune's jades.

But no longer are we subject to his laws
since we set a questing foot on Jove's dry land,
naked newts evading Ocean's gaping jaws,
leaving dreaming, saw-toothed terrors to the dark.

Stoutly, boldly, we defy the sea-green spray,
flinty, glinting, slingshot pearls of rainbow ice,
and we pick our steady, steadfast, holdfast way
down the rugged, ridgebacked, granite dragon's spines

Till we reach the homely, horny house of light
where we burn a warming fire of seasoned oak,
warning of the earthly men who come by night,
breathing sour, musty air still sharp and dank.

Green Sheep

They need to be watered, need to be fed,
need to be numbered, cropped and bred,
need to be given light and air,
need to be given love and care,
need to be saved from flood and drought,
need marauders, thieves, kept out,
need to be labelled, listed, dated,
sorted, sprayed, checked over, mated,
so that we can eat their offspring,
russet, pippin, scrumpy, codling.

Green

Leafy green, village green, bowling green, putting green.

Pea green, sea green, starboard green, eyes of green.

Spring green, eat your greens, go it's green, gone green.

Bottle green, battle green, Lincoln green, olive green.

Grey-green, Goose Green, Saint Stephen's Green,
   Winson Green.

The Girl in the Picture

You see the girl ogling a thunder-cloud,
adoring her god, the indwelling saint?
Uncaring, he seems, unshakeable, proud;
she has his blank eyes, his virgin restraint.
Her right hand points to her undefiled heart,
her robe is as chaste as the new day's dew,
cleanly as any in Renaissance art.
I reach out to touch the Marian blue.

But look again. Is she pure as fresh milk?
The dress is slipping from shoulder and thigh
while loose gathered rumples of textured silk
and a bare left arm lead the vulgar eye
to a valley below her gibbous breast
which promises more than heavenly rest.

Art Gallery

And do you remember the kid on the bed
who was facing away with her bum in the dead
centre of the frame?
We admired the lines, the use of the glass,
the curves and the tints, and the light and shade.

And then we saw
the stone-dead birds,
the storms at sea,
the broken columns
and the fleeing souls,
the landscapes carpeted in snow.

And we looked about at the same old men,
obliging nymphs and crumpled crones,
and families wearing fancy dress,
and martyrs tied to trees and shot,
and bathing girls and belted earls
and knowing women in hats.

End of the Pier

Our childhood is sinking,
rusty, crusty, shameful piles
with knobbly, contorted knees,
aching for the past,
for bloaters and boaters
on the carousels.

The canker is spreading
up their old-time dancing limbs,
the strollers with varicose
maps of easy walks,
their thin, green-lipped mussels
and their empty shells.

They're dreaming of bandstands,
ups and downs and round-abouts,
of Floss with her candy and
Penny in the slot
who sent coppers chasing
after bathing belles.

The legs long for bracing
mufflers, caps and winter coats,
the shelters are howling and
painted wavy blue,
the chips now are gambling
and the sewage smells.

While shiny new motors
line the glitzy promenade,
the cocktails, the dives and joints
serve the idlers right,
and it's bookings only
at the posh hotels.

contd...

So watch out for hazards,
trips and trippers, turning tide,
approaching the end of the
jaunty, gaudy pier
undone by the backwash
from the rousing swells.

Blue

Navy blue, rowing blue, Oxford blue, boys in blue.

Eyes of blue, baby blue, Royal blue, Prussian blue.

Small blue, common blue, smutty blue, filthy blue.

Lips are blue, hands are blue, toes are blue, noses blue.

The Admiral of the Blue knows no fear.

The Admiral of the Blue brings up the rear.

Sailing

When we were round and smooth
and we dabbled in the waves,
the bearings were unknown to us,
the journey was a holiday,
the ocean open wide.

When we grew strong and lithe
and we took the helm ourselves,
our parents lolled astern and smiled
while we set course for Paradise,
where youth and wealth reside.

But when a child was born
and our hands were occupied,
we rigged a jury sail and left
the steering to the wiser ones
until they ailed and died.

Then we were cast adrift
and the boat roved where it liked,
the false horizon tacked and yawed,
and we lost all control without
our forebears as a guide.

Until we saw the lights
of a distant winking shore,
consulted charts and shortened sail,
and knot by knot passed on our skills
to hands as yet untried.

But skylines slewed once more
when a grandchild joined the crew,
the heavy swell rose mountains high,
the harbour lights drew far away

and skipped from side to side.

And now though limbs are stiff
and the sails are tough as hide,
the rudder is a trunk of oak
and spars weigh more than anchor chains,
we once again preside.

But soon our captain's berth
must be handed back to youth,
and we shall lie at rest and dream
of when we were once strong and lithe,
and thought we knew the tide.

Waterfall

Growing older's much like rowing,
gazing back at where you've been,
not ahead at where you're going:
brief encounters, narrow misses,
pairings, partings, curses, kisses,
flotsam, jetsam, wrecks unseen.

I have used my seven ages
skimming rapids, reefs and rocks,
looking out for landing stages,
dodging floods and whirlpools, punting
in the weedy shallows, hunting
quiet water, quays and docks.

But I've only sculled a sliver
of the web of western streams:
with its blue-veined arms the river
stretches way beyond the mountains
to the youthful springs and fountains,
and the foothills of my dreams.

Nowadays my pace is slacking
and my beat's erratic, slow.
Will is strong but strength is lacking,
I am losing way, misjudging,
finding every effort grudging,
in the turbid, livid flow.

For I've left the heady reaches
of the sparkling, fairy source,
and mosquitoes, flukes and leeches,
sudden shivers, weirs and rip tides,
rockfalls, branches, brickbats, landslides
plague my daily zigzag course.

But downstream lie darker places,
and I shall soon see them all:
creeks and slipways, roaring races,
salty burns and brackish marshland,
misty harbours, mire and quicksand,
when I cross the waterfall.

Beyond the Station

Walk up the lane not far beyond the station,
where once a girl child wandered full of grace,
and you will find a woeful habitation,
a mournful, bleak, dilapidated place
where still she lives, a faded, fallen elder,
a bruised and pitted Ellen Let's-not-name-her.

Some folk have two legs, and some folk have four,
and four legs seldom are as sore.

Such wizened words she'll toss at folk who ask her
what made her give the house away to beasts
while once it throbbed with music and with laughter,
with Christmas parties, summer galas, feasts,
and she will say that animals have features
humaner far than many fellow creatures.

Billy at the upstairs window,
Dobbin snorting at the down,
Daisy in the best front parlour,
Porky in a silken gown.

Climb up that bluebelled hill beyond the station
to where she lodges windblown all year through,
refusing neighbours' help and conversation,
devouring cow-cake, columbine and rue,
her eyes still raw from fires no longer burning,
remembering, regretting, smarting, yearning.

Some sores are stubborn, and paradise hides
the ugliness of rural rides.

Indigo

Light indigo, deep indigo.

Code Indigo, Air Indigo.

Mood indigo, woad indigo.

Time to go beyond the blue.

Our Orchard

So God be praised for dappled things, for Gerard Manley
    Hopplekins,
for rosy, ruddy, wrinkled, bloody, spotted, scruffy
    crumpleskins,
for scabby, dumpy, cankered, lumpy, hearty, tarty pippinkins,
a squeeze of which makes rosy cider, scrumpy cider,
    kilderkins.

For shrivelled, stillborn plums and peaches, withered
    damsons, whiskered quinces,
walnut boats with broken beech-masts, elderberries, fallen
    cherries,
Worcester pears as hard as conkers, bottom-heavy like some
    punters,
silken, naked mulberries and desiccated apricots.

Each one of them has fungal growths that mar and scar the
    morbid skin,
and mistletoe that taps the sap within the haemophilic limbs,
and caterpillars, aphids, beetles, sawflies, midges, wasps and
    mites
that sponge upon the leaves and buds like fawning, crawling
    parasites.

Yet they survive, the Handsome Norman, Doctor Hare's and
    Ashmead's Kernel,
Williams', Bon Chrétien and Comice, Rivers' Early, Laxton,
    Monarch,
not just apples, pears and plums but cousins by the score, the
    hundred,
keeping bloodlines going, growing, lest a weakened branch
    should rot.

Descended from the Tree of Life, each has its honoured yard
    of ground
within the orchard with its share of sun and rain and holy air,
for each is sacred, serves its purpose, teaches us to take and
    eat
the fruit of wisdom, bitter wisdom, mellow, galling, sour,
    sweet.

Windflowers

We are, as we walk through a woodland glade,
distracted sometimes by a shaft of light
that javelins through the lazy, lilac shade
and strikes upon a silken bed of white

where windflowers lie, their petals open, splayed,
among the pithy stems that stand upright,
and stepping from the path before they fade,
we gaze with idle longing at the sight.

We bend perhaps to pick a sparkling bloom,
to clutch it to our breast, before we see
we can still love it if we give it room,
and knowing where to find it, leave it be.
We climb back to the path, which is as straight
as lines upon a score, as strait as fate.

Six Seven Three One...

The colour wheel's six,
red, yellow and blue,
with the o-g-p in between,
while the arc is seven,
the highway to heaven,
where lightning gods crackle and reign.

And prisms split light into red, green and blue,
converging again into white.
So light can be three
and light can be one,
which those who know can explain.

But though the pigments red, yellow and blue
can produce every tone, every brash man-made hue,
there is yet a different kind of white
which is white as whitewash, white as lies,
and shades to black, black dyes and eyes,
black ink, black drapes, black looks, black ties,
through a thousand intriguing shades of grey
that cover the cracks and are seldom quite
as pure as it says on the tin.

Violet

Violets are red and violets are blue.

Violets are variegated too.

Scented violet, gentian violet, morning violet, evening violet.

Yin and yang and violent violet, invisible violet, ultraviolet.

Who knows what lies beyond the blue?

Beyond the Spectrum

Beyond the spectrum are secret suburbs
where colours vanish and cloudy contours
of photoelectrons float and flicker,
infra within and ultra without.

Inside, the airwaves idly loiter,
broadcasting blindly in slow-worm bandwidths,
lazily crawling across the cosmos,
longer and longer, looking for life.

But in the ultra-violent outside
short waves grow shorter, shifty and pint-sized,
poking their noses in private places,
X-rays tearing through tender pretences,
gamma rays gate-crashing guilty pleasures,
squalid, unseemly and out of sight.

Belief

Garden Paths

Who is that in the shovel hat
and broad expanse of bombazine?
It is my late great-grandpapa,
born in eighteen-fifty-something
in a world of bassinets,
of flannelette and bayonets
and please, God, save the Queen.

He sits immobile, mutton-chopped,
his chin close-shaved, tight-stocked, severe,
his hands clasped on his aproned lap,
fiercely contemplating nothing
with a ridge and furrow stare,
upright and square, a high-backed chair,
inscrutable, austere.

A massive cross hangs on his chest,
enough to rip the toasting fork
from Satan and his fallen friends,
Bible on a covered table,
heavy, handy, solid, squat,
with which to swat the slightest jot
of risqué rustic talk.

My grandpa wears a different set
of sombre dry-as-dust attire,
stiff neck, stiff collar, morning dress,
joined the Revenue, pursuing
frauds and liars, still a true
believer who, in Sunday pew,
addressed a God of fire.

My father followed in his steps,
a functionary who received

inherited respect but spent
Sundays building bonfires, weeding
fruit and veg and flower bed,
or in his shed and never said
how much he still believed.

And I have walked a rambling path
of dead ends, ditches, brambles, doubt,
sometimes well-lit, more often dark,
stumbling, fumbling, collar rumpled,
cross and fork befouled with rust,
the mind non-plussed, the flowers dust;
the fire is all but out.

Roming

I'm thinking of joining the Church of Rome.
I'd like to share a Sabbath home
with saints and incense, lacy graces,
candle grease and smiley faces,
psalms and charms and friendly laughter,
folk who're certain what comes after,
bells and smells and genuflection,
all the bling of self-deception.
Bless me, Father, I have sinned.
All do, son, it's in the wind.

Or maybe I'll stay as I am
and keep the message simple
without the immaculate misconception
or the implausible resurrection.

Railway Hats

Like hats abandoned on a moving train,
the questions who and how and what and why
are left when we alight, and they remain
unanswered, never mind how much we try
to make sense of the scenes that pass us by.

Ask me how many and I'll run the stats
of tunnels and turn-outs and sewer rats,
of journeys begun and guides I have bought,
but ask how to fill up the empty hats,
and the answer will always end in nought.

Dürer's Four Horsemen

Four steely assassins are squatting on haunches
in mushroom sun by a scrimshaw sea,
swapping stories of shipwrecked sailors,
Noah, Odysseus, Aeneas, Canute.

They are playing a permanent game of poker,
their hands well hidden in hollow chests,
deciding which card to slap on the shingle,
how each will harry the holiday crowds.

The savage in grey says he'll scorch them to cinders.
He'll toss an old stub in the scrub and he'll smile
as sparks fly spinning to caravan sites,
and watch as the wind turns the demon wild.

The bruiser in blue says he'll send them to blazes.
He'll drag them from sunbeds and down to the deep,
and leave behind layers of plague-sodden land,
of sinking foundations and slurry and slime.

The gargoyle in green says he'll give them a snorter.
He'll snuffle and slobber and gob out his spittle
at jostling, jackanapes, jaunty invaders
on gimcrack, congested, jerry-built proms.

The bandit in black says he'll march them to battle.
He'll laugh as they fight local folk over food,
he'll lay waste their homes, their harvests and harbours,
despoiling their fishing smacks, forges and farms.

The wreckers are restless and ready to roister.
They leap on their four-by-fours, level their lances
and surge through the woodcut spreading disaster,
fire storms, flood tides, infections and wars.

Picking Sides

The free enterprise pilgrims
are hunting rare earths
on the right side
of the ribbed planet.

The self-righteous unity commune
is established on the
left and is already
stripping it to bone.

The bubble-wrapped clumsy earthlings
wave their sharpened shovels,
shouting vacant slogans towards
each other's matching shadow.

Until a dying prospector
clutches in extremis at
the left and right
chambers of her heart.

The Numbers Game

Pick a number between one and plenty,
add n thousand and times it by twenty,
which is the average number of rows
of patients waiting, how long no one knows,
like lambs in the pen with its threefold gate:
pasture or sheep-dip or straight to the plate.

Next count the jobless, the businesses failed,
the tests, the ops, the treatments derailed,
the kids not learning to reason or read,
the number abused, the number in need,
suicides, breakdowns and mental distress,
and draw a neat graph of the whole damned mess.

Then place in the scales your totals, ignore
those you think faulty, and see which weighs more,
rounding the sums up or down as required
till you reach the answer that you desired.

Maud

I see you standing by the garden gate,
your face a silver dollar, eagle-bright,
half-smiling, body radiating light,
translucent, lace-winged, bleached, attenuate.

I beckon, but you falter, hesitate,
and so I go and take your hand, and sense
the press of flesh on flesh, alive, intense;
I pull you to me, feel your heart pulsate.

You are no ghost, no lover once betrayed,
no vengeful phantom spirit; you exist;
I saw you here this afternoon, we kissed,
and yet you are a memory, a shade.
And what, I ask, can such a vision mean
for grander apparitions some have seen?

Cloister

In the beginning was the word,
the breath that gave life to the Earth
and stars.

On your left is the library,
its wisdom penned in shackled books
shut fast.

And on your right the study cells,
where words gestate and reproduce
unchanged.

And everywhere the fog of prayer
drifts up like smoke from smouldering fires
of faith.

The gate is closed, but warming room,
and parlour and refectory
are bright.

So rest content: your words and songs,
your silences, sustain the world
outside.

Yet one injunction: do not touch
the tree of life that dominates
the garth.

Its tempting fruit is out of reach,
for ordered minds an arcane branch
too far.

AD 410

Severus stands surveying his four-square domain
and seems to glimpse among the crippled orchard trees
the turtle-plated legions of his glory years
when arguments were simple, iron-bound and keen.

He knows that he is seeing old men's wistful dreams,
for those brave eagles who once beat their swords on shields
and fathered heroes fell for Rome on foreign fields,
while codling youngsters of today would shun the fight.

He lost his son in what were called defensive wars.
For what? he asks, when now rebellion spreads like fire
and green-eyed former enemies have landed on
the open shore and spread their rooftrees far inland.

His daughter is betrothed to such a Saxon knight,
a decent man who understands the laws of Rome,
the language and religion, but who still pursues
within his hidden heart a harsher alien creed.

Severus has some sympathy, for he preserves
for old time's sake a set of ancient household gods,
a clutch of dusty kickshaws, clumsy figurines,
inherited embodiments of racial pride,

While on his chest he sports a leaden Christian cross,
and though he does not take the Gospel word for word,
he argues that it holds the world together and
is no more baseless than the ancient myths.

You must hold fast to something, he reflects, as he
pulls tight the plaid around him in the autumn breeze,
the plaid adopted long ago from people who
once occupied the very hillside where he stands.

How the Stones Came to the Northland

Within the washpot of our inland sea
where flesh and fish and olives, corn and wine
appeased our idle bellies we perceived
Your greatness only dimly by our thumbs,
for on the frigid, fiery mountain peaks
and by the mumbling, lipless springs and streams
of sunrise, mid-day, midnight marching lands,
we failed to heed the meaning of Your arc.

We knew to shun the shaded forest bounds,
the burning desert wastes and fetid marsh,
to live within the limits that You set,
but when the wind propelled us far beyond
the sunset gates into the Ocean's void,
where nightly You dipped down to still Your thirst,
we trembled and implored Your present aid
to lighten our befuddled eyes and minds.

The sages told us we should not return,
but driven by the tide we ventured on,
like mountain lions marking with our sweat
each headland, crag and eyrie that we passed,
to honour You, observing Your descent,
encouraging Your rebirth as the source
of life and love and law, and to exalt
Your termless going out and coming in.

It was no easy task to pitch the stones,
to grave the leading lines at high and low,
to hew the timber, build the ramps and bring
the massive weights from where they split and fell,
but every spire we stood upright on downs
revealed a moment more of unseen light,
Your declination growing shallow till

one night You did not sink to rest at all.

As we went further, knowing we were close
to understanding how You roll the year,
we saw You sleeping longer once again,
regaining strength as chilling moontides passed,
maintaining night and day of equal worth,
the balance that we mortals need to thrive,
and we described with thanks on alien shores
Your everlasting round of death and life.

Basic Arithmetic

A zillion stars per galaxy,
a trillion or two of them
per visible physical intraverse,
and topsy planets waltzing around
with conkering moons and little green men.
They say the numbers are baffling.
No, they're not. They're finite.

How many squares of my toast are magic?
Number and cut into crumbless chunks,
and rearrange them until they add up
sideways, slantways, crossways, all ways,
upways, downways, always the same.
Multiply 142857 by the figure 3.
Result: 42857-1.

Count your breaths, your giggles, your paces,
count the times you stir your tea.
Keep an account of the words you utter,
and add one more if they're odd.
Divide the length of a string in half
and half and half and half and half:
Measure the world with your fingers.

Statue

I see an opaque, foursquare granite base
as hard and smooth as when the block was found,
and yet the sculptor's vision seems to trace
Prometheus within, impatient, bound.

She sees a head and shoulders and a face,
a prodigy emerging from the ground,
stretching, moving, occupying space,
the granite changing shape, elliptic, round.

I close my eyes and I too think I see
a breaking wave within the solid block,
a wriggling something struggling to be free,
to break out from the gravid, deep-veined rock,
the shape of change, renewal, fragile earth,
the shape of love, of life, the shape of birth.

The Medieval Seasons

Winter began on November the first,
All Souls' Day, Samhain, spirits and saints,
Hallowe'en homilies, mystical kennings,
half-way between the equinox
and the Christmas dip of the solstice,
embracing the turn of the screw of the year,
with feasting and forfeits and stashing of food,
fodder for beasts that would earn their keep,
slaughtering of the remainder.

Spring began when the ewes' milk came,
Saint Brigid's Day, the first of Feb,
Purification and lambing and Light,
the Imbolc stories and poems retold
upon the Lupercalia,
tales of wisdom and healing and what
was learnt from grieving and breaking the ice,
from beasts in the byre and the bleating of friends
over the candle-lit winter.

Summer began with May Day games,
with maypoles and Morris, remembering martyrs
on hands and knees on the highest hills,
with Beltane beacons burning all night
and holy wells with haloes,
with running and jumping and archery butts,
with prayers for sun and warmth and rain,
Hazel and Primrose with flowers in their hair,
nothing but beans in their bellies.

Autumn began on August the first
with dancing and prancing at Lughnasa,
with berries and cherries, the earliest fruit,
the glut of the gardens and cutting of corn,

and tasting the first of the cider,
with jesting and joking and coming to terms
with rivals and neighbours in echoing barns,
preparing the Lammas mass of the loaf,
thanking the Lord for the harvest.

So vivid, so fitting, when tied to the year,
the times of abundance, of starving and hope,
and always they knew that you cannot sow seed
where ground is hard-hearted and stony.

Normality

It is normal to learn the names of wild birds,
of mammals, of insects, amphibians, fish.
It is normal to listen to Mozart and Brahms,
to study the piano or violin,
It is normal to act or to play in a band,
to read, to draw, to make sculptures or sing.

It is equally normal to live without books,
but with kind parents, kind neighbours and friends.
It is normal to lie on the sofa and bat
back and forth hilarious juvenile texts.
It is normal in summer to sit on a beach,
play football and music, laugh and raise hell.

It is normal to be left alone for a week,
and fed on take-away scraps from the bin.
It is normal to hear that you get in the way
and to suffer from bruising and broken ribs.
It is normal to think that the rest of the world
is quite unaware that you even exist.

Faith

The total truth will never be known
of who were Zoroaster, Moses, Mani,
the Buddha, Jesus, Mohammed, Rama,
Guru Nanak or Joseph Smith.
Add whatever names you like
of prophet and preacher,
interpreter, messenger,
punisher, ravisher,
seer and soothsayer,
conjurer, questioner,
blusterer, sufferer,
arbiter, pardoner,
victim and vanquisher,
judge and condemned.

Do the historical details matter—
birth and death and weeks in the wilderness,
friends and enemies, forerunners, followers,
whens and wheres of wild revelations,
who said what to whom and why?

Is not the overall message more meaningful—
earthy, empyreal,
quietist, pietist,
contradictory, claiming victory
over death and cycles of misery,
laying down rules for treating properly
people you happen to meet on the street?

Ought you to treat them with zealous severity,
cut out and burn apostasy, heresy?
Or should you welcome them, jolly them, coddle them,
show them how loving, how kindly your worship,
offer them comforting sayings and sandwiches,
give them the neighbourly warmth of your fellowship,
tell them, some things you don't need to believe?

The Garden House

The plans are fine, show what is meant.
The Architect sits back content:
his grand design is cunning, neat,
the project carefully thought out, complete,
a heavenly experiment.
The bloodshot bricks, the sand, cement,
instructions too, have all been sent
to build the couple their retreat.
The plans are fine.

And yet for all his good intent
the work is lagging, rules are bent,
foundations crumble in the heat,
uprights and cross-trees do not meet
despite the time and thought he spent.
The plans were fine.

Family

For Esther

When you glance at the photo's frosted face,
I hope some curiosity remains.
A trickle of my blood beats in your veins,
and I once ran the same uneven race.

I always liked my quiet, private space,
for which I fought obtuse, zigzag campaigns,
a pinball bouncing off life's rude chicanes,
evading, dodging would-be friends' embrace.

I shall not know what path in life you take,
but if, like me, you tend to hide your tears,
your joys, your disappointments and your fears,
I beg you for my overcautious sake
to turn to friends instead, to trust to those
in whose eyes loving kindness plainly shows.

Faithful

Faithful to mother, to refrains she taught me,
to quavers and rests in the quickening womb,
for who is not faithful to mother, whose tears
dribble on down through the dirge of our days?

Faithful to father, to the saws he brought me,
the dusty old score that he understood,
for who is not faithful to father, whose themes
linger like blood on the stave of our brains?

Faithful to school, where we learnt about cheating,
the playing of parts and keeping in time,
and faithful to friends, despite changes of key,
modal shifts, dissonance, catches and lays.

To first love, the skylark still singing, still grieving,
the endless repeats and bass viol lies,
to last love, the never-more turning of sheets,
dominant, tonic, organic, sustained.

Footsteps

Whoever is dogging my footsteps is cunning.
When I stop, they stop moving as well,
and when I resume my morning run
their gravelly, shuffly, twig-snapping steps
again fall in with mine.

From time to time I spin round so quickly
I catch a glimpse of angular shapes,
hear echoes, laughter, undertones, sighs,
indefinite sounds that I cannot make out,
and names from long ago.

I think of the people I know I offended
who might still bear a black-and-white grudge,
a selfish but justified sense of wrong,
a weight they might want to dump at my feet
to spoil my latter days.

Are they truly wandering, unquiet spirits,
remembrancers whose task is to tie
a ball and chain to my scurrying heels,
or are they purely imagined regrets
created in my mind?

The only way to lose them is to stand stock-still,
be conscious of blood flow, heart rate, pulse,
inflate the airways, breathe through the nose,
reflect on the failings that cause the malaise,
and say a silent prayer.

Uncle Rundle

I remember waking to seagulls squalling,
black-clad widows talking, squawking,
Uncle Rundle, who said nothing.
I remember still the river wriggling,
Clarinda for ever refilling the pot.

I remember someone's cottage perching
on a hillside, scented bedding,
counting bobbing trawlers creeping
into harbour in the morning,
I remember waking to seagulls squalling.

I remember scowling fire-tongs, trying
not to cry, and smells of frying
fish with hideous heads on, meeting
old men mending nibbled netting,
black-clad widows talking, squawking.

I remember with my parents going
to a bigger house and eating
scones with great-aunt Bessie, seeing
my great-uncle sitting nodding,
Uncle Rundle, who said nothing.

What, I wondered, was he thinking?
But they said his mind was flaking,
worn by years of heating, quenching,
beating, rasping, smelting, brazing.
I remember still the river wriggling.

His old forge these days is serving
so-called Cornish teas to passing
trade but I remember tasting
scalded cream like fudge, and helping
Clarinda for ever refilling the pot.

Plough Yard

In the cheery firelight glow and tobacco smoke
The bargee and the Ludstock carter share a joke.
By the frozen trough outside, in her plain homespun,
The carter's only daughter meets the bargee's son,
     In the Plough yard, boar-and-sow yard,
     Canal-and-Severn-trow yard.

In the leather and the oak of the private bar,
The sexton and the rosy parson share a jar.
In the stable with the oxen, on a bed of hay
Are Tom and Kit rejoicing in an older way,
     In the Plough yard, I-and-thou yard,
     My-goods-I-thee-endow yard.

In the skittle alley, watching the ninepins fall,
The bargee and his scion lounge against the wall.
In the shadow at the side-door, by the off-sales sign,
Is Kitty waiting, waiting in the Lent moonshine,
     In the Plough Yard, furrowed-brow yard,
     The chilly-breezes-sough yard.

In the entry, rolling tuns of West Country Ale,
The carter shivers, knowing what it is to fail.
In the draughty, dirty jakes with its broken staves
Is Kitty holding back the unrelenting waves,
     In the Plough yard, laden-bough yard,
     A-child-I'm-getting-now yard.

In the heavy door-shut closeness of the sombre snug
Sits Kitty with the cunning woman's sworn-by jug.
Through the horse-muck slithers Tom, who is fancy-free,
Away to Bristol docks and boundless life at sea,
     In the Plough Yard, how-oh-how yard,
     The heaven-can't-allow yard.

In the quiet of the private, empty mugs set down,
The parson and the sexton nod and sigh and frown.
On the cobbles of the entry, trading blow for blow,
The carter and the bargee battle toe to toe,
        In the Plough Yard, bitter-row yard,
        The roving-keel-and-prow yard.

In a corner by the chimney, with her glass of port,
The cunning woman counts the coins she took for naught.
In the creaking cart of empties, bitter taste still there,
Is Kitty jolting homeward to the Mayday fair,
        From the Plough Yard, broken-vow yard,
        Before-my-fate-I-bow yard.

Thieves

Here's to the thief who stole my work
to save himself the bother,
here's to the Artful Dodgers, trained,
who dipped me in the Forum,
to the skinny man in need of a meal
who nicked six quid from my office,
to the father and son doing purses in Prague,
the cruising Hamburg bicycle thieves,
the antique dealers who bought the stuff
extracted from family houses.
And here's a double dose of dope
to the yellow rat who sat on his tail
and cribbed my credit card numbers.
Let it go, let it go.
They know, they know.

Scattergood's Yard

He's solemn is Scattergood, solemn and slow,
But he understands horses, he hears what they think.
He tells from the teeth what old terrors they've seen,
And his fingers can feel faded scars in their flanks.

He'll sell you a shaft-horse, a Suffolk or shire,
Or a hack or hunter for Tom when he's home.
He'll find you a cob for young Colin or Kit,
Or a stout Shetland pony for Sally or Sim.

He's gone is Will Scattergood, safe underground
With his brother from Bridge Street, the brazier's sons.
Yet still there are stables beside the old cots,
And old stories are stored in the whispering soil.

The breathing and snorting of beasts is still borne
On the warm evening breeze as it blows round the yard.
The odour of hay and the sweet heavy scent
Of hot horse-mash still hang in the humid night air.

You'll hear the clinking of harness and hooves
If your ears are attuned to continuing time.
At dawn and at dusk you'll detect if you look
A long sliver of shadow that's solemn and slow.

For solemn was Scattergood, solemn and slow,
But he understood horses, he heard what they knew.
They told him what terrors and times they had seen,
And he felt every flutter and twitch in their flanks.

2020: The Worst Year of Our Lives

In many ways it was the worst,
when parents and siblings, companions and pals,
soul-mates and strangers, sickened and died,
when wages dipped and dripped and dried,
when joy was crushed in the jingoist jaws
of crass, bombastic, back-room bilge,
was skewered by genocide, sacrificed, scarred,
and spitted on spiral statistical spikes.

A year of despair and suffering for scores
whose minds were twisted, tortured and torn,
who curled and crouched and cried alone,
wretched and robbed of their reason and lives.

Yet I also remember old moments of mine
when I wandered a weary and featureless waste,
heavy-laden, alone and lost in the fog,
aware I was walking the wrong stupid way
up the wrong stupid road from the wrong stupid place
with the wrong stupid people, wrong prospects and plans,
dejected, rejected, a jester who frowned
and spoke to a silence that hung like a shroud.

But I have since learnt a few lessons from life,
have tested and tried, retracing my steps
till I found the right partner, right purpose, right path,
and could feel the enfolding affection of friends.

Found

here's a slender silver plaything
from the age of inky ledgers
of the inst. your valued orders
humble much obleeged remaining

copper plate predating typing
but look closely and discover
there's no nib nor no lead neither
so no earthly use for writing

but relates somehow to clerking
found among the rolling rulers
sealing wax and spills and tapers
of my Great-great-uncle Harding

it is hollow cracked and gaping
like his photo on the dresser
nothing but a tarnished silver
spineless gutless empty casing

My Shadow

I bury my misdeeds five fathom deep,
the sufferings for which I am to blame,
omissions and commissions and a heap
of petty selfish thoughts I cannot name.

I think of them each night before I sleep,
the foolishness of which I am ashamed,
the perfidies, the downright crimes that keep
my dreams in turmoil and my mind inflamed.

They weigh upon my shoulders like a sack,
a cumbrous, clumsy burden on my back,
I glimpse its shadow as I walk the street,
though others make no comment when we meet.
Perhaps because I often see a face
suggestive of some similar disgrace.

The Five Senses

The senses all diminish with the years,
although his taste in wine is more advanced
now he can buy the better, dearer kind:
well-being, health and temper much enhanced,
his hearing sharpened too so that he hears
the words his children say but try to hide,
and silent heavy footsteps drawing near.

And as for her, her touch remains as strong;
despite the shrinking of her road-mapped hands,
a lightning charge still flows from heart and mind,
while clouded eyes now let her understand
the things that puzzled her in times long gone,
when left alone she clutched her knees and cried,
aware the world smelt rancorous and wrong.

For Sophie

I shall not know you when you are a teen
for I shall be an empty cockleshell,
a childish trinket on a shelf, washed clean,
beside the Russian doll, the Swiss cowbell,
and magic stones from by the Holy Well.

But if you choose to hold me to an ear
and close your eyes and listen you shall hear
a distant breaking voice you may recall;
and it will quell the storms that then appear,
just as it calmed the waves when you were small.

Old Age

Morning is Broken

Each morning when I first look out I see
an origami line along the hill,
a frieze of cut-out shapes like Santa Claus,
their hands and feet conjoined, outstretched and still.

They are of course a row of ancient trees
arrayed in silhouette against the sky,
a parley of old bones, a dance of death
whose interwoven branches trick the eye.

And in among the limbs are darker squares,
like blackened windows draped against the night,
or crenellations on a castle wall,
where men-at-arms stand to, prepared to fight.

Above them rise the long-armed, porcine snouts
of engines that will hurl down rocks and fire
on night-capped burgesses in panelled rooms,
on peasant, serf and freeman, lord and squire.

Then sunlight strikes the ridge, as though a match
were struck among the trees, a careless spark,
a second and a third until the hill
is pock-marked with the flames of burning bark.

There is no sound, I only see the flash
and sense disturbance in the muggy air
as through my window streaks a silver lance,
projected from some demon's choking lair.

The walls around me shatter, split and fall,
the desk, the chair, the books are torn apart,
and in that mortal moment of release
I feel the final flutter of my heart.

A nightmare? No, each morning's waking dream,
a presage of unwanted, wanted war,
until the trees in daylight are revealed
for what they are and peace prevails once more.

Eld

The rower is old now, arthritic, reaching
for a drowned-out past improbably perfect,
catching crabs in Dupuytren claws,
weary with world-pain, worried by sores,
recking succeeding surges and spills
as the darkling days and the dreamtime draw in.

Around him the rigadoon dinghies are reeling,
slipping and snaking through slow-moving surfers,
mermaids, monsters and misleading lights,
babbling and burbling in bath-time fights,
heeling in spiralling circles of spit,
enjoying their juvenile jousts with the skiff.

But the revellers, he reasons, will soon be reefing,
heading for home and the fish-net harbour,
sparing sinews that strain and ache
as sheets and shrouds start to shudder and quake,
shortening sail when the sun grows dim,
when the grim clouds gather and the chill begins.

He watches them rest a while, wryly reading
the incipient signs of slackening pleasure,
wondering whether eternity will
go on for ever and how he'll fill
unending empty hours as he ships
his oars and sits, and smiles and sits.

Just Passing Through

Just passing through, at a café
I paused to pass the time of day.
'We're friendly here, indulgent, kind,'
the waitress said. 'If you've a mind
you could extend your holiday.
Or settle here, why don't you? Stay
and pick the rosebuds while you may.'
But I could not, though much inclined.
Just passing through.

Then decades later, old and grey,
I happened to go down that way
to where the café was, to find
it gone, and what remained behind
a heap of ashes, dust and clay.
Just passing through.

Villa Nell

Do you remember Villa Nell,
the house in France we sometimes took?
I do remember very well.

Where comfrey grew and chanterelles,
and garlic that we used to cook.
Do you remember Villa Nell?

You loved to watch the pipistrelle,
and otters playing in the brook…
I do remember very well.

…with stone and weed and oyster shell,
and we would sit for hours and look.
Do you remember Villa Nell?

We lazed and drank the muscatel
while borage waved and bedstraw shook.
I do remember very well.

But now such things have lost their spell.
You poke the fire and read your book.
Do you remember Villa Nell?
I do remember very well.

Harvest Moon

The soil was once a springy, yeasty gold;
it ran through fingers like the sands of time,
rewarding back-bent labour sevenfold,
eternally renewed each year, sublime.

But now it is a cloddish, spreading mould,
a clinging, squelching sludge, a stinging lime,
the scar-faced harvest moon bloodshot and old,
sunk hollow-cheeked in unproductive grime.

The scarlet coats, the Yankee Blue, the Gray,
the camouflage, the twill and padded stuff,
cockades and orange sashes, khaki, buff,
have merged into a mess of lumpen clay,
while high above the pharaoh's gaudy barque
shines down upon a sightless sea, wine-dark.

Zwei-sprachig-keit

They say two-speaky-hood holds back the onset
of—qui quae quod quis quid?—dementia.
In which case I am still patently mented,
waking to find myself muttering speakies
stuck to my juvenile corkboard with Sellotape—
cortex, corticis, masculine—learn it,
five times a week.

First came the unfenced vowels of farming,
of muttons and beefs and porkers and canards,
Jean who loved football and Jeanne who loved Henri,
followed by heroes observing the unities,
drivellers, dribblers, counting their syllables,
tragical-comical troupes of immortals,
Attic, antique.

And then the optional extra, the otherspeak,
spouted by Harold instead of by William,
Schiller and Goethe and Heine and Hofmannsthal,
hiking through pastures and pine woods and history,
whinnying black letter freighted with destiny
offspring of margraves, arch-dukes and emperors,
goblins and trolls.

Straight-backed hidalgos who spoke like machine-guns,
swallowing S's along with the miracles,
smoother and sunnier children of Dante,
ending each phrase in a dew-dropping vowel, or
consonant clusters of babushka bouncers, who
fill in a record of every encounter,
earning their doles.

Learning the fragments, the pleases and thank-yous:
price of the oranges, how much the couscous?

Language the only conceit I was good at,
seeing the structure and hanging the vocab
on Ararat's peaks and the ruins of Babylon,
sacred intentions and secular statutes,
tangles of law.

Now in the two-speaky evening of consciousness
talking in twinklings of Teutonic wakefulness,
seeing things sideways, still playing at double-think,
other words borrowed from Empire and enemies,
shooting like stars in the emptying memory
jottings of this and that scribbled in folders
locked in a drawer.

Dead Villages

Dig and you shall find, they tell us.
Dig round here, you'll find dead bodies,
men and women, beasts of burden,
tillers, reapers, orphaned children
clutching rusted playthings, ploughshares,
harness, hay rakes, cauldrons, armour,
bones unhallowed, huddled, harried,
ghostly memories of hamlets
lost to plague and wars and tractors.

Dig among them down to bedrock
and you still won't find a village
with a pub, a church, a baker,
parish pump, the post, the grocer.
Now in rural Hampton Ducis,
Thorpe Episcopi and Regis,
neatly laid to tar macadam
you will only find Duke's Orchard,
Bishop's Crescent and King's Acre.

Where the carters trudged the byways,
where the hayward counted trusses,
thatchers wove bouquets of rushes,
hedgers, ditchers, poultry keepers,
shepherds, cowherds, milkmaids, cotters,
rose in darkness in all weathers
and the women took in outwork,
wearing out their eyes for farthings,
there is no such aching labour.

Now folk need degrees in farming,
agronomics, water, land use,
DNA and engineering.
Work for most is driving bargains,

office, laptop, tablet, mobile,
but for those who long for colour,
blues and greens and earthy textures,
those who once preserved the landscape,
driving vans is what's on offer.

Words

The words are hiding in the underbrush,
whispering silliness,
susurrating, sibilating
sibyls making sly remarks,
gagging the giggles and
stifling screams.

I can hear their twopenny, tittery squawking,
tee-hee chattering, nattering, talking,
I observe their tipsy, tottery walking,
tittupy, trollopy, tip-toe stalking.

The teasing words are promiscuous, lush,
promising glorious
new editions, fresh commissions,
poetry prizes, readings, cheques:
sirens that sing to me
in my dreams.

The Gloucester to Hereford Canal

Come along, gents, I am offering you shares
in a bran-new canal with bran-new locks
to bring you your coal and your vital stocks
of tools and machines and Brummagem wares,
to pick up your cider, apples and pears,
your Comice and Conference, Cwmmy and Cox,
and take them to market, to Gloucester docks,
tuppence a ton, any time, anywheres.

The parson, the judge, the colonel, the squire,
invested their pounds and shillings, the fools,
in navvies and barges, horses and mules,
till a monster breathing out steam and fire
swallowed their savings and laid its hard road
on the bed where their quiet water flowed.

Waiting Room

I am propped up in a dimly lighted room,
watching the candle gutter in the wind,
waiting to enter the next compartment
where the light, they say, will blind me.
Dazzlement or outer darkness,
one extreme or the other.

Sit there please, where I can see you
a little, in my good eye,
and talk to me of shopping trips,
of cabbages and things,
of anything you like that will
break the cheese-dome silence.

And I shall quietly riffle through
my old address book, wondering where
everyone now is.
In my mind, you understand,
since they claim I cannot see,
or hear or taste or touch.

But I can see the white-winged dove
dipping, diving, climbing high,
and don't forget that hearing stays
when other senses go.
Be careful therefore what you say;
they'll bring you tea if you ask.

Asbestos

In memory of Alec Letchford

This is where they breathed the foggy
snow-flake filaments and fibres,
clinkered, slow-built coral sinkers,
bleached white bones of old companions
flocking just beneath the surface,
sucking breath from dead-sea drifters.

This is where the fireproof jackets,
warm as toasties, toasted toesies,
made them cosy, nosy, throaty,
wrapping him and her and kidders
in a coat of scaly blubber
like a pair of bedroom slippers.

This is where the sharpened needles
stuck like burrs of pricking thistle
in the anchored sheets and ticking,
hiding in the lungfish rigging,
turning chokers sides to middle,
caulking itchy-scratchy scuppers.

This is where they keep the trolley,
tubes festooned around the capstan,
oxygen that lets him dabble
in the dusty drowning ether,
counting down the time remaining,
nursing rotted ribs and timbers.

Cauli

Don't tell me, don't tell me,
I know who you are,
I just can't remem—
Put in your password.
That's easy, it—Ah.
Enter your PIN code.
Have I a PIN code?
Hold the thing steady,
can't see the right-hand
edge of   the map.

The caterpillar has been grazing on the cauliflower.
The cauliflower is a floret short of a Waitrose.
The cards are tipped all over the floor,
face up, face down, some slipped through the cracks.
Picking them up will take a while,
stacking, sorting, right-way-rounding,
storing, knowing where I've stored them.

The cauliflower has been bitten by the caterpillar.
The caterpillar has been sectioned,
as is seen
on the screen.
A nod and a poke
from the bony old bloke
in the cowl and the cloak
with the blunt-edged scythe
who has nipped off a tithe
of your cauli.

And yet
the florets are sending out new tendrils,
twining, combining, retwining, reshooting,
chemical composted cuttings rerooting,

going off route, circumventing the shell-hole
where the unguided electrical missile
happened to strike,
the patch where the cat has
demolished the pillar.
Fill out another card for the index,
name and number,
hold it where I can see it.

A Stroke of Good Fortune

Lost words, crossed words, crosswords, cross words,
algebra never made sense to me,
roots weren't square but tangled,
offering homes to hodmedods,
pricklebacks and mouldwarps
tucked up warm in quilts of leaves,
patched and matched and batched and thatched,
clubs and spades and ache of hearts,
diamonds and rubies

Dried words, tried words, dyed words, pied words,
wriggling out from underneath,
germinating, ideating,
bubbling, boiling, spitting, soiling,
oily, ruddy, roily, bloody,
opals, garnets, bloodstones, jacinth,
gems of livid usquebaugh
caught like hanging dewdrops, long drops,
flailing geese and boobies

Piled words, filed words, mild words, wild words,
mimed and primed and timed and rhymed,
blenched and trenched, belied, besighed,
waiting for the whistle blow,
crawling up the downward slide,
tumbling off the fairground ride,
limping, primping, purled, cockeyed,
holed, resoled, resold, resouled,
ancient clods and newbies

Known words, flown words,
buried hoards of no-man's land
flung out at a stroke

Music Remains

I have no idea what you're gabbing about,
I'm not even sure what relation you are.
They say I am losing the plot, if there is one,
which I most earnestly doubt.

My auricles, ventricles, varicose tentacles
can still recalibrate, pencil the distance
yet to be travelled on wings of a dove:
how many Beethoven quartets and symphonies,
how many times round the Ring of the Nibelung,
how many times I shall see Calaf's sun rise,
how many times the High Priest will cry Traitor!
before Radamès is entombed?

While conversation may now be cacophony—
often enough it already was sophistry,
anomie, hominy, filling the sandwiches—
music, my music remains.

Nine Lives

I have survived near drowning
when they told me it was shallow and it wasn't,
a fractured skull
when I braked to avoid a pedestrian
and sailed like an unfledged albatross
over the drop-head handlebars,
a burst appendix,
which was just a pain
till the grumbling grew to fever pitch
six septicaemic weeks later,
a head-on collision,
seen coming, seen coming, seen coming and—bang!
angina that had me
walking and talking
like Timmy the tearaway tortoise,
a brace of brain-freezing,
tongue-twisting,
one-sided,
right-minded
strokes,
and a gob-smacking, chest-banging heart attack.

It looks as though
there is one life to go.

Three Strokes and You're Out

at the third stroke
remember that?
you're much too young
the speaking clock
you could dial this number
from anywhere
and ask the time
and it told you to
the nearest ten
nine eight seven six
five four three two
one—
seconds

not a lot
but worth a shot
drag it out
tick by tock
time to take
your pills and stock
of all the things
you never did
and some you did
and shouldn't have

Autumn

The limbs are foxed and mottled, brittle, spare;
they shiver in the tilting rain,
the springtime urging gone, the crown now bare,
the nerve-ends numbed, the senses dead.

Young fleshy growth has hardened, split and dried,
vermilion glory fallen, shed,
while fruits that swelled are scattered far and wide,
and only shrivelled nubs remain.

Rest quiet in the ground, await rebirth
upon a better, bright spring day,
eternal life, a whole new heaven and earth,
is what they say. What some folk say.

Bredon Hill

From here you see the soft swell of Bredon
where ploughboys and their belles once peeled and lay,
Trojan horses snorted boustrophedon,
and churches blest the sowing in the hay.

By Severn, Avon, Wye, Teme and Leadon,
bowing, whispering elders pine away,
dreaming of a slow, caressing Eden
when they ploughed the old Arcadian way.

This is a gilded, long-remembranced land
of fecund soil, a golden book of hours
where Celtic sylph and new-age settler meet,
where sturdy, cross-bred, long-limbed saplings stand
and Shropshire lads go picking fresh spring flowers
and lay them down in the burgeoning wheat.

Reviews

A Colourful Age by Peter Sutton brims with musicality, a wry sense of humour and sometimes tender, sometimes acute, reflections on the world and its ways. Sutton manipulates his skills with language to underpin his themes, deploying questioning, alliteration and chiming rhythms which give pace and energy to both personal and political poems. He says '*I am walking around the rim / gingerly minding where I put/ my feet*' but I would say that his feet are placed firmly in the poetry of pace and rhythm. Here are elements of Frost, Manley Hopkins, Auden (*Night Mail*). The writing is reflective and playful yet still politically on point as in *2020: The Worst Year of our Lives*, and in two beautiful heirloom poems to his grand-daughters. These honest, generous and wonderfully diverse poems will touch many readers.

Tina Cole, winner of the Yaffle Poetry Competition, 2020

Peter Sutton's *A Colourful Age* is a multihued reflection on life's impermanence in which he throws a 'javelin of light' onto humans and humanity. Split into four quarters, Colour Vision, Belief, Family, and Old Age, the whole is an accomplished work including astute observations of attitudes to modern-day living. He questions right from wrong, left from right, faith under a 'fog of prayer', and ponders on our data-driven society through the need for a 'Tomato Licence', in a straightforward, witty, no-nonsense style.

These poems can make you smile, make you cross, make you wonder and catch at your heart. They are rich with rhythm, rhyme, alliteration and musicality. Read them out loud, savour the sounds.

Lesley Ingram, winner of the National Stanza Competition, 2020

In this collection of superbly crafted poems, Peter Sutton connects you to a rich seam of people, places and stories. From urban settings such as *End of the Pier* to the rural mood of *Autumn*, he creates lines that resonate with folk-like rhythms and benefit from his exceedingly rich vocabulary. His use of alliteration, as in '*A cumbrous clumsy burden on my back*' from *My Shadow*, harks back to medieval poetry.

Although studded with stunning sonnets like *Bredon Hill* and *For Esther*, his poems embrace a wide range of other subjects and forms, from a pub in *Plough Yard* to the Renaissance painting in *The Girl in the Picture*, all of which is leavened throughout with works of wry humour. A very entertaining read.

Clifford Liles, author of 'The Thin Veneer', Dempsey & Windle, 2022

Thanks

Black Pear Press published my short collection *Elgar Country* in 2022, and I would like to thank them for their continued confidence in my work, in particular Polly Stretton for her detailed and sympathetic editing, and her colleagues Tony Judge and Rod Griffiths for their helpful queries and comments.

My involvement in poetry began a decade ago, when I wrote a presentation about William Langland for the Autumn in Malvern Festival. Without that initial invitation from Peter Smith, Artistic Director of the Festival, none of the poems in this or any other collection, nor indeed my translation of *Piers Plowman*, would have been written.

In the intervening years I have been further encouraged, challenged and educated by speakers at poetry workshops, audience members at readings, editors of poetry journals, and members of groups including Accent on Poetry, the 'Hereabouts' Herefordshire Stanza, Ledbury Poetry Festival Salons, Worcester LitFest Speakeasy, Malvern Writers' Circle, and the Worcester Libraries Poetry Bubble. I have read some of the poems in *A Colourful Age* to these groups, and I am grateful for members' suggestions.

My reviewers are drawn from these groups, and I thank them for their willingness to give me their time, and for their kind words.

I also thank the publishers of the handful of poems in this volume that have previously appeared online or in print: Ledbury Poetry Festival, Herefordshire Stanza and Sarasvati.

About the Author

Peter Sutton began his poetry career with publication of his modern alliterative verse translation of William Langland's 7500-line medieval poem *Piers Plowman* (Jefferson, North Carolina: McFarland, 2014). This was followed by *Poems of Armenian War and Peace*, jointly written with Liana Hayrapetyan and sponsored by an Armenian cultural trust (Yerevan: Edit Print, 2019).

His suite of poems *Mayflower 1620*, a compilation of his own words and poetry of the period, was belatedly performed in Malvern in 2022, with music chosen and performed by the Gaudeamus choir of Gloucester.

And in 2022 Black Pear Press published 27 of his poems under the title *Elgar Country*.

Some 30 other poems have appeared in the journals *Acumen*, *HQ*, *Orbis*, *Poetry Salzburg Review* and *Sarasvati*, online or in anthologies, and a few of them are republished here.

Peter has given readings from *Elgar Country*, *Piers Plowman* and other work at conferences and poetry festivals in the US and the UK, and he frequently appears at West Midlands poetry events. He was joint winner of the 2021 Kipling Society John McGivering Poetry Prize.

His plays *Elgar and Alice* and *The Prebumptious Mr Punch* were premiered in Worcester, in 2007 and 2013 respectively, and his translation from German of Rolf Hochhuth's *Death of a Hunter* was first seen in London in 2018.

He has edited and translated numerous books, articles and reports for international organisations, lawyers and arts centres, and is a former Head of Publications at the Unesco Institute for Education in Hamburg. He has written and spoken widely on languages, Elgar, Langland and poetry, has written German language textbooks, and has been a visiting lecturer at universities in Armenia, Germany, Russia and the UK.

Acknowledgements

I am grateful to the initial publishers of the following poems:

'Dürer's Four Horsemen' was first published in Ledbury
Poetry Festival, *'Lockdown Poems'* project, (2020)
'Statue' was first published online in Herefordshire Stanza,
'Vision' project, (2020)
'Plough Yard' was first published in Herefordshire Stanza
pamphlet, *'In Plain Sight'*, (2016)
Scattergood's Yard' was first published in Herefordshire
Stanza pamphlet, *'In Plain Sight'*, (2016)
'For Sophie' was first published under the title 'For my
Granddaughter', *Sarasvati No. 065, June-August,* (2022)
'The Gloucester to Hereford Canal' was first published in
Herefordshire Stanza pamphlet, *'The Waters of Herefordshire'*,
(2019)
'Bredon Hill' was first published online in Ledbury Poetry
Festival, *'Ledbury Hills'* project, (2018)